Marie-Claire Di Carlo

Catechism

Marie-Claire Di Carlo

Catechism

The Catholic Faith

Blessed Hope Publishing

Imprint
Any brand names and product names mentioned in this book are subject to trademark, brand or patent protection and are trademarks or registered trademarks of their respective holders. The use of brand names, product names, common names, trade names, product descriptions etc. even without a particular marking in this work is in no way to be construed to mean that such names may be regarded as unrestricted in respect of trademark and brand protection legislation and could thus be used by anyone.

Cover image: www.ingimage.com

Publisher:
Blessed Hope Publishing
is a trademark of
International Book Market Service Ltd., member of OmniScriptum Publishing Group
17 Meldrum Street, Beau Bassin 71504, Mauritius

Printed at: see last page
ISBN: 978-613-7-84709-1

Table of Contents

Finding Jesus

Jesus is found in the temple.

Even the best of parents Mother Mary and Joseph lost Jesus. They found him in the best place ever after looking everywhere., in church. And so let that be a lesson to all of us that when you loss Jesus in your life go to church you will find Him there, teaching and preaching through our priests and laypersons that serve our Lord's house. The House of God is open to all the children of God to find Him and bring Him with you wherever you go and carry Him with you all the days of your lives.

In church you can find Jesus in the Eucharist during mass and physically have him present in you, the Bread of Life, all the days of your life. When I returned from Jerusalem I went to the Oratory everyday and even before then but when I returned I ate nothing else but Jesus rarely but I did have an outside bite, Pa's birthday, my birthday, coffees, lots of coffees. I only started eating in prison and in the hospital, had to I was obliged to eat, but Thank you God for food but Jesus is the true food from heaven. My health results were ok almost 3 months of just having Jesus. Doctors will be upset with me but I truly believe that Jesus kept me alive with no sickness all the time. I was diagnosed with a relapse of my bi-polar but Jesus physiologically kept everything healthy all the time.

I recall Jesus saying these words once, whatever you have done to the least you have done to me. We are children of God and in each of us God gave us divine gifts and qualities and we have a piece of Jesus with us. So loving one another we are called to finding Jesus in one another as well. We must love our enemies too because Jesus died for everyone and that's why his example of love is for all of us to love one another.

We can also find Jesus in Scripture, in the Old Testament and the Bible. Back then they only had Scriptures and many found Jesus this way like the wisemen.

Exorcism

Jesus in the Bible, casts out demons, and sends them into pigs that went over the hill and drowned. He also cast them out people. He commanded they leave and they did. These are what we call today Exorcisms.

There has been Saints which were able to cast out demons like St. Francis Brogia. He was a Saint from the 16th century and it was said that as soon as he finished praying the evil spirits would leave. Saint Anthony of Egypt from the 1st century was also known for casting out evil spirits. He was tempted daily by the evil spirits but his Holiness prevailed. St. Benedict form the 1st century as well. He was known to cast out the devil with the sign of the cross. St. Peter the Exorcist from the 1st Century was known for his exorcisms in Rome. He is even mentioned in the Canon of the Mass. Lastly Saint William of Toulouse was known for his spiritual direction and exorcisms in the 14th century.

There is a list of Catholic priests that perform exorcisms. Since Jesus was able to cast out demons he handed over that power to his Apostles. Therefore priests should be to all cast out demons. Exorcisms are performed around the world. If ever you encounter an evil spirit in someone get a Catholic priest.

Dec 8th

Immaculate Conception, All is New!

The birth of Mother Mary was like a rebirth of the world. Her birth gave a second chance at humanity to redeem to God. She is Holy and God chose her to be the Mother of God, Jesus Christ. An angel Gabriel came to announce this news to her and she gladly accepted God's mission to save the world and use her to fulfill His divine plan for God's salvation and be a mode for women and mothers everywhere to surrender to God's will and give everything to him and everything He makes is great and wonderous. Mother Mary was conceived late by her parents Joachim and Anna at a late age, God's plan has no age but in his time He does great things. Mother Mary was made at a later age and in her youth, pure age, God made her the handmaid of the Lord and Mother of our Savior.

Her Yes to God changed everything for humankind. Born was a hero, a Savior of our Lord whom guided us back to Him who created us. His ways was God's ways and we had the perfect example to be reborn and remade in Christ to follow to God. He taught surrender to violence, he taught peace instead of war, he taught love instead of hate. Mother Mary was part of God's great plan to save the world and that little baby born on Christmas day so innocent and pure was born of the Holy Spirit and God gave us his biggest gift on that day, his son Jesus who loved us to death. He came for us, He stayed with us, He died for us, how great is our Lord, Awesome!

Mother Mary, emblem of great faith, teacher of faith, she believed that God and her faith in God brought us all closer to God. Her faith moved us to believe and keep believing in how wonderous God's love is for us. She knew from the beginning how Great God is, He knew how sacred, virtuous, pure Mary is and was to be and bestowed her with the highest virtue of being our Savior's mother. And even though we killed her son she knew it was for the salvation of our sins, Jesus in great faith gives us Mary as his mother, as one Holy Mother. And what a Great Mother she is, was and always will be.

Jesus - a Lover and a Fighter

Jesus took the beating for us. He underwent the 14 stations of the cross for us. He proved His love for us and God's love for us. He wants us only to believe and follow Him. He fought for us by dying on the cross for us and He won.

Jesus the lover not in the sexual term of the word but in that he chose to love above all. In all his actions and words there is love the resounding sound and the act. He loved us to death that is why I consider him a lover and fighter.

His resurrection is the win He aspires from all of us. He is the living God, in Him there is life. Who believes in Him will never die and so we must keep our faith strong, like rock. The church is the rock Jesus left behind to follow in his footsteps and to keep in great faith believing in the resurrection every moment of our life.

Jesus teaches us to fight, anything in His name will be granted in great faith. Also, He gave us the tools to fight evil by prayer and to not be afraid. His words teach us God's love for us. His actions of preaching and teaching he has passed on to us and His church to keep spreading the Good News. His actions of healing and expelling demons he has passed on to those with great faith and the apostles that made and build His Church.

Marriage

Genesis 2:24: "Therefore a man shall leave his father and his mother and hold fast to his wife, and they shall become one flesh."

These days, many have forgotten this quote from the Bible about marriage. There is so much divorce that many are discouraged to marry to end up the same. In Canada alone, there is a 38%-41% chance of divorce.

Marriage is a mystery and it is a sacred sacrament in the Catholic Church. It is a mystery how 2 people fall in love and find themselves at an alter in front of God vowing to love one another in "good times and in bad, in sickness and in health. To love and honor all the days of their lives as long as they both shall live." Many that have their parents together dream of having a similar luck in their love life. Others whose parents have divorced dream of finding someone that they can love forever. Just because your from a broken home doesn't mean you will end up the same way.

What qualities make a great partner? Definitely, the faith has to be there. Sometimes it's what brings you together. God brings you together for the purpose to love each other and one day bear children and raise them in the same faith that brought you together. What are the secrets to a long happy marriage? I am not married but I was told by my parents caring, compassion, understanding, communication, trust, faithfulness, and mutual respect. The late John Paul 2 quoted about marriage, "Marriage, the Sacrament of Matrimony, is a covenant of persons in love. And *love can be deepened and preserved only by Love,* that Love which is "poured into our hearts through the Holy Spirit which has been given to us" (*Rom* 5:5)."The Holy Spirit may be who guides you to your love and helps deepen that love throughout the years.

Why do people give up too soon? When arguments arise there is always the hurt that follows and forgiveness is necessary to begin anew. Sometimes pride gets in the way of reconciling. That's why pride is such an ugly deadly sin.

Loving someone forever is not only easy but its romantic. Imagine you met your love young and you're the only love they have ever known and you grow old together until one dies then the other dies later on and you reunite in heaven again. But this kind of love is rare. Many nowadays have fallen in love many times until they find the one they want to share their life with. Along the way there is hurt and broken-hearts until true love prevails.

Remember that marriage is not about 2 but 1. One flesh thinking together, feeling together and growing together and you'll be one of the lucky ones that last a lifetime.

Marriage Part 2:

Since I was little I was taught that marriage is a sacrificial and selfless act. Let me explain.

My grandmother at the age of 20 married my grandfather at the age of 23. It was right after World War 2 in a little town of Italy called Pietracatella. There was no jobs which forced my grandfather and a few other men in the town to emigrate to Venezuela for work. And the sacrificial life began. My father was just born only 3 months when his father left to provide for the family.

My nonno (grandfather in Italian) would send money back to my grandmother by mail every few months, then finally an opportunity struck in Canada for him. So my grandmother with her 6 year old son (my father) came to Canada to be together. My grandmother got pregnant again and had my uncle and then they decided to return to Italy and raise the kids there. My nonno stayed in Canada and kept sending money to provide and support the family.

When my father was 10 years old my nonno asked them to return to Canada and make a life there. That was the last time my father saw his beloved Italy as well as my grandmother and my uncle Michael. They came to Canada and Canada became their home. In total my nonno and grandmother were separated from each other for 12 years and all during the beginning years of marriage. This, to me, is a deep representation of sacrificial love.

Then there's the selfless love. When a union is made nothing but death can separate them. It's over 20 years that my grandfather is dead and my grandmother still wants to celebrate their anniversary as though they were still alive. Even after death their love lives on, its romantic and special and I wish to meet someone that makes me feel that way too someday.

The selfless love I speak of was when my nonno was sick and everyday my grandmother would make him his favorite food and bring it to the hospital. The leukemia was aggressive and got my nonno in 3 months. He died so young at the age of 67. I sometimes think that more could've been done to make him live longer but I was too young to understand. The selfless act of love, of loving another more than yourself and making sure they were OK I witnessed with my grandmother in those hard days. My uncle used to drive her everyday to the Montreal General Hospital to see him and bring him "home" food.

With my parents on my mom's side I saw another selfless love act. They used to every night put cream on each other's legs, it was nice to see. My grandfather had a difficult death, he suffered psychologically and physically and his kids had to transport him wherever he needed to go. When he died, I witnessed my grandmother being very lonely and missing him a lot. When your other half leaves you, you feel half whole.

Then there's my parents an ultimate example of sacrificial and selfless love. My parents have been married for 38 years now and their love keeps on strong. But they have had their challenges over the years. In the beginning there was a lot of misunderstanding and fights due to it. But towards their 15 year anniversary my mother became sick, she had a mental illness. It took her a while to seek help but when she did my father was by her side, supporting her along the way along with her 2 kids, myself and my brother Anthony.

It was a sacrificial few years that followed since my father had to take care of my mother and since we were still young my mother was taking care of her children the best she can considering the obstacles she faced. Having a mental illness slowed everything down. She felt tired due to the medication and had to push herself out of bed and to do her chores. It was hard but eventually she was back to the way she was several years later just on medication now. She is still on medication and can do everything she used but she needs her medication to stay "normal". My father was there for her throughout those years. It's almost 23 years now that she has been sick. Even when my father wasn't well she'd take care of him, even though he is suppose to take care of her. That's the selfless love acts that accompany them throughout their marriage. I wished that my mother would be cured from her mental illness but in God's time.

I'm not married but looking at the example of my parents and grandparents I have learned what true love looks like and how love can last. The Church helps of course. My parents got married with the Catholic Church and raised us to follow tradition and example of Christian love. My grandparents were raised with the Catholic Church and taught their kids likewise. But what for the generation of today? Is marriage still the same as it used to be? Is there the same kind of sacrifice and selfless love acts that used to solidify marriages? I hope so.

I am not married but I can tell with my friends that are married that have just bought a house that lots of sacrifices are being made. No vacations, cutting here, cutting there, the list is endless and especially when they are expecting a baby, Madonna, the expenses seems endless and the gift of life so precious becomes a new journey of sacrifice for both parents together.

But more and more couples are looking to live together first and have children and marry later why the reverse? Simply said marriages are expensive and saving up for one can be a sacrifice in itself. I long for those days of our grandparents that had a simple, inexpensive wedding, and started their lived humbly together. Nowadays not only do young people want the BIG wedding but also the BIG house which requires lots of saving up, forgetting our grandparents route. Our grandparents sacrificed their lives to give us a better life. They didn't buy the house right away they saved and put money aside until they had enough for a home.

Do I aspire to marry in today's day, yes! I had great examples of love in my life and I wish to meet someone that makes me feel the same way. I had the opportunity to marry someone I loved but I wasn't ready then. I truly loved him. He went on to marry someone else and has a child with her. I regret my decision many times but I guess destiny is this way. I hope he is happy and experiencing all the joys of marriage and may the sorrow moments be not so bitter. I cared for him in a selfless way as I left him to be free with where he wanted to go with his life, whether or not that included me. I was sacrificial because I lost him to another and deep down its my deepest regret of all this.

I have a childhood friend getting married this year. It's the BIG wedding and they bought a BIG house to live in afterwards. I pray for them. They have known each other for over 5 years and now have decided to unite. I wish them well, they never lived together before, they went traditional that way. I hope their marriage last a lifetime and they have many children and that they are both ready for the sacrifices and selfless acts that their marriage will require.

To sum up, love is the most beautiful feeling we experience in this life. And when we share it with someone else how much sweeter is that. But love requires sacrifice as Jesus Christ showed us in His eternal sacrifice for us. Love is selfless and sacrificial and I have witnessed these acts in my grandparent's relationship and my parents'. I aspire one day to be in a relationship as well, with the maturity of my ancestors, and hopefully be married as well. But we have a whole life to be married, the important thing is to marry the right person. The one that will bring out your desires of sacrifice and selfless acts. How do you know you've found the right person is a whole different topic that I hope to discuss with you again. I'm still searching, it's an ongoing search for us singles but there is no rush. Better off being alone than with the wrong person. And there is no rush to marry there is no age but if you want to have children than of course earlier marriage is required since us women have a time frame to have children. The important thing is marrying for love and being ready to sacrifice and give selfless acts.

Miracles

Miracles happen everyday, before our eyes around the world. Sometimes it's God telling us he still loves us and heals us, sometimes it's Saint's intercession that cure us. Sometimes it's Mother Mary telling us she is still with us and haven't abandoned us in her messages to us. Miracles are the impossible made possible through the intervention of God. They increase our faith that God still loves us and is by our side.

Saint Joseph of Cupertino had a difficult time with his vocation but finally became what God wanted him to be a Franciscan priest. It was witnessed that 70 times when he was praying or saying mass he levitated. That is why he is the Patron Saint of air-pilots. Only God can levitate us.

St. Padre Pio was another well known Saint of the century and a Franciscan priest. He performed many conversions and many healings but he is well-known for his stigmata that he bore for 50 years. He had the same wounds of our Lord! That showed God was with him through that miracle.

St.Clelia Barbieri died young at 23 years old. She told her religious sisters that she will remain with them always. A year after her death a voice can be heard in the choir that sounds harmonious and they believe it is her voice still participating with the nuns. God is truly present.

Here in Montreal we have a saint that lived and healed. It's called the Saint Joseph Oratory and his name was Saint Andre. I am a witness to the miracles performed in that church. I was hemorrhaging for almost 2 weeks in a row. I decided to go visit the Oratory and when I left my bleeding stopped. It was a miracle!

Ask for miracles through prayers and they will be granted to you. Or ask the intercession of a Saint. Visit Holy shrines and sanctuaries where miracles have occurred and maybe your miracle will come true.

Mother Mary, Appear to Us Again

Mother Mary has been known to appear to us in numerous occasions throughout the world. In those sites usually the Catholic Church declares them sacred for the apparitions and many cures have been attributed to the site. I wonder what The Virgin Mother Mary would give us as a message today? To allow women to be priests, for priests to marry? Who knows.

Our Lady of Guadeloupe is a special case in the 16th century in Mexico, she appeared to Juan Diego (Saint) to convince the Bishop to build a church where she appeared. After much refusal from the Bishop she finally performed the sign that convinced him of her presence. She appeared to the Bishop on a tilma with roses. She is now the patron saint of Mexico and a cathedral was built in her honor. An incredible list of miracles and cures are attributed each year to the site.

Our lady of Lourdes is another case from the 19th century in France, where Mother Mary appears to a young girl by the name of Bernadette (Saint). She shows Bernadette a hidden spring in Lourdes and asked that they build churches where she appeared and hold processions. Lourdes is known for its healing powers many go there and are miraculously cured. The statue inside a cave she is referred to. Recently a French nun was healed at the site from her spinal complications. She was wheel-chair bound and now she can walk!

Our Lady of Medjugorje appeared in 1981 in what was then former Yugoslavia. She appeared to 6 children with messages to pray and help the lost. There were apparitions with the Mother and her infant child. There was apparitions of a spinning sun and rosaries turning gold. The signs are to draw us to conversion. There has been testimonies of brain tumors that were healed and many other physical healings.

Early in the 20th century there was Our Lady of Fatima which revealed herself with a message to 3 children in Portugal. She appeared to them every 13th of the month from May to October and in October 13th she appeared to many through the sun. The sun was dancing that day! Even our beloved Saint Padre Pio was cured by our lady of Fatima. One day her statue was visiting various spots of Italy and she found herself in the presence of a sick, bedridden Padre Pio and she healed him!

We ask that Mother Mary renews our faith and appear again in the 21st century. A time when we are so skeptical and our faith withers at times let her appearance strengthen our faith and bring new hope that she remains with us always.

Saints

Holy people are called Saints. Usually someone becomes a saint after they die. Someone puts in a nomination for the person's sainthood status and according to how they lived they can become a saint. Also, they can become a saint according to what they do after they have passed on. It takes 2 miracles to make someone a saint. First, the person is blessed then they are venerated and then they are canonized by the Pope. Anyone can become a saint in the Catholic Church but they need to believe in Jesus and that He is the Messiah.

An example of a living saint was Padre Pio a renowned Italian saint. He prayed 39 rosaries a day, listened and forgave thousands of confessors, he had the living scars of Jesus' wounds, the stigmata, and was known for being in 2 places at once. Saints are holy people that the Lord blesses with special gifts of healing and miracles.

Saints can become saints after they have passed on too. Monks, nuns, abbots, holy people are kept in churches and if a miracle happens where their body is found after death then they are venerated and if another happens then they are canonized to prove the saint is still alive, listening to our prayers and interceding on God's behalf to help make miracles happen.

Saints are not idolatry since we are always praying to Jesus and the Holy Family. They are special people chosen by God to intercede because God listens to the prayers of the holy and grants them in great faith. Anyone can become a saint, it is a master of the perfection of prayer and discipline of self and a mastery of faith. Jesus said anything asked in his name will be granted, saints have perfected that the proof is in their faith and the actions that follow. St. Pope John Paul 2 said it first, "Do not be afraid to become saints."

St. Joseph the Carpenter and The Father of Jesus

St. Joseph is great! He is a descendant of David destined in God's plan to save His people. First David saved his people by fighting against Goliath and then Jesus saved his people from sin. St. Joseph was a humble man and God made him so great. He is the saint of Canada and the father of our Savior and Lord, Jesus.

Angels had to guide St. Joseph to God's plan. First the angel Gabriel appeared to St. Joseph's dream to tell Him of God's plan with Mother Mary and Jesus. When the baby was born an angel appeared to Joseph to guide his ways to Egypt with the Mother and child to protect them from King Herod. Angels then appeared to St. Joseph to tell him when it was safe to return back to Nazareth. Angels also appeared to Mother Mary to ask to be the Mother of our Lord, Jesus. Angels are always guiding the Holy Family and so they guide us in our daily lives to know what is good. We all have guardian angels.

St. Joseph's occupation was a carpenter and we learnt that even our Lord Jesus took the same occupation as his father, humble, obedient servant of our Lord. St. Joseph guided Jesus throughout his life to live God's ways, to be an obedient servant of the Lord. His example molded and shaped Jesus and helps us follow in his footsteps of loyalty, devotion, humbleness, obedience to out great Father in heaven.

Adoration

Every church has a moment of adoration.

When they place Jesus in the monstrance and we adore his presence and sacrifice for us. He is the miracle worker and feeling his presence brings healing and peace and love.

Saint Clare, my saint, she used the monstrance to avoid a war that was nearing. Miracles can happen and adoring our Lord can only reap positive experiences and feelings.

Adoration is also used when looking at the Nativity manger. We essentially can not go back in time yet however we can be taken to the moment in history, that changed history, when Jesus was born. We can be like those adoring shepherds that angels appeared to to announce the Great News that happened in Bethlehem. Or like the 3 wise men that came from far to adore the born Messiah. From far and wide adoration brings us closer to the One that came for us, to save us, to show us the good way to God.

Jesus Our Shepherd

The Lord calls us by name. We trust him, he calls us his little flock. He never abandons us. When we are lost he comes to find us. He is the Good Shepherd that will always protect and defend his sheep. We recognize his voice. He wants us all in heaven with him.

Jesus the miracle worker

Ask me anything in my name I will grant it. During our most darkest hour or moment we need to just pray to Jesus. It is when we suffer that we rely on God more and ask for his healing. He wants us to depend on him always.

When we suffer we cling to Jesus and he who suffered for us is with us always.

He can heal anyone at anytime just ask and just pray. Jesus is the best person to have by your side, the bestfriend, he loves us unconditionally and wants us to love him the same. He wants us to have confidence in him, to believe in him, and to trust him with his timing on things and healing and keep asking. He came to heal us from our sicknesses and forgive us from our sins. How happy we are when he heals us and gives us what we've been asking for a long time, joy springs from our hearts.

Jesus is joy! Angels rejoice when he is around! He is always there and always cares and shows his love for us in our lives through healing and miracles. All great things God is behind it. He is that Awesome!

Jesus, best guy to have at a party, he keeps the wine coming and the joy pumping. He loves us so much and is crazy about us and wants only that we believe, stay faithful, continue the work he has done and keep praying.

Apostles, Disciples, fighting for Jesus

Jesus, our Savior and Redeemer died for us. His love for us went beyond death. He came back to tell us we don't die but will resurrect as well thanks to Him and His Father, Our Father God.

Knowing this we can only fight for our faith as well. Fighting does not mean physically all the time but if need be Jesus took a beating for us we can only return the favour if need be ever. The Apostles followed his footsteps and all gave glory to God's love for us through them. Martyrs and saints have also brought great glory to God's Holy names through their actions and great commitment and devotion to our Lord Jesus.

His promise is eternal, He is always with us and never lets us down and even in our darkest hour when we feel most alone, afraid, abandoned, he carries us back home to Him. He, we love and he loves us so, completely with all his heart. His name is great, He is great so we must fight to keep our faith strong, our love to endure forever like His and our mind, body, and soul directed to Him and what he needs of us in the world. I love the song Make me a Channel of your Peace by St.Francis.

Jesus was simple and sacred. In that simplicity He created everything in great faith with Him he can do anything we must, as he said, just believe. Mystery that blows my mind, the breaking of bread and fish. I would love to see that miracle today. The greatness of God to distribute to everyone. I wish I live to see this miracle done because there are so many poor, disciples hungry for God.

Baby Jesus

When you see a baby think of baby Jesus. He was so small and helpless and he came into this world to save us. That's why Christmas is so important it's his birthday and instead of receiving gifts we exchange gifts with our loved ones, all thanks to him.

Holy family, Santa Famiglia

When a family is in trouble it's great to turn to the Holy Family for guidance. Mother Mary, St Joseph and Jesus are a model family. They are holy and always listened to God and led their lives according to God and have been greatly glorified because of their sacrifices. They are simple and humble people and very obedient to the Lord.

God's plan for them that Jesus have wonderful, loving, holy parents, who'd love Him as their own. He was God's son. Angel Gabriel announced it and guided their ways afterwards knowing that King Herod was not pleased with God's son to be born to save his people from sin.

The Holy Family respected the laws and presented Jesus at the temple where they were greeted by Simeon who was told her see the Savior, before going to heaven. Luke 2: 28-36. God always keeps his promises and keeping his promise to save us we have Holy Parents, Mother Mary, Joseph and Jesus our Messiah.

Luke 2:41-53, all parents make mistakes. Even our Holy Parents, Mother Mary and St.Joseph lost Jesus in Jerusalem. Luckily after looking for 3 days they found him in the temple preaching in His Father's House. With great faith Jesus came to reinforce our faith. From small he knows his mission and he completed it 3 days later. His parents found him and whenever we are looking for Jesus the first place to look is in God's house. You will always find Him and the Holy Family there. God bless you and keep you close to Him!

What the Holy Family asks of Us?

We celebrate epiphany Jan 6th of every year to commemorate the Holy Family. In South America it's called the 3 kings when the wisemen presented gifts to Jesus. The Holy Family is a gift from God.

Mother Mary is the obedient, humble, bridesmaid of the Lord that gave birth to wonderous Jesus our Saviour. She sacrificed her reputation to follow God's command knowing that the community would probably have her stoned to death for accusations of adultery, and great faith knowing that she was innocent and God would protect her and keep her safe and He did.

An angel appeared to St.Joseph in a dream to reveal the truth of God's Holy plan for them and he rejoiced knowing that God was sending forth His Savior and that he, humble and obedient St.Joseph would father Him. In Italian tradition we celebrate St.Joseph on March 19th. It's a big feast: we celebrate the Holy Family and we have zeppoles and 13 plates of food and someone dresses up like St.Joseph, another like Mother Mary, and another like Jesus. It's a wonderful tradition that we do to commemorate their Holy presence in our lives. St.Joseph is also the saint of Canada and in Montreal there's the Oratory built in his honour, it's called the St.Joseph Oratory and many cures have sprung forth from there. It was built by St.Andre and many people visit from around the world. He fathers us and guides us to Jesus. Mother Mary in her holy virtues, protects us and leads us to Jesus, and consoles our hurts and pains since she had suffered much in her life, she is the model of empathy and love and is blessed of all women.

Jesus our Saviour born as a baby came to bring us great news of God's salvation and everlasting love for us. Born humbly in a stable and they had no place in the inn except there. We need to let them IN our lives and hearts to show us God. They came to guide us and show us the way and we must follow. Just as the wisemen were guided by David's star, so must we follow the Holy Family from Jesus' birth to his death in great faith of the resurrection. They came to show us the way, we must simply follow humbly and obediently, like them, the way of the Lord.

Prayer

Prayer is our way of talking to God. He listens to our prayers, as well as the saints and Mother Mary and Jesus and the Holy Spirit, and answers them. But sometimes it takes years, sometimes it takes days to answer but they get answered in God's time. You just have to be patient.

Why do we pray? To stay close to God, to ask him for things and favors, for guidance, we pray for healing, for others to heal, and for others. There are different prayers that you can say. You can recite the rosary which is a prayer that consists of mysteries 53 Hail Marys, 6 Our Fathers, 6 Glory Bes and an Apostles Creed and begins with the sign of the cross. There are also prayers like My Guardian Angel which is usually said at night before bed. And grace before meals is also a prayer.

Nuns and priests spend their whole day in prayer. That's why they have a special relationship with God. Many become saints.

You can pray anytime and anywhere, God is always listening.

So pray and may all your prayers be answered.

Jesus and Communion

The Last Supper was the moment Jesus gave His body and blood as a sacrifice for our sins and as a remembrance of what He did and we do it every Sunday. Jesus transforms himself into the bread and wine as His body and blood to nourish us.

There was a miracle that was performed in Luciani, Italy. A priest doubted the miraculous transformation and suddenly the bread turned into real flesh right in front of his eyes. The communion makes us one with God. Just as Jesus and the Father are One so we are with God when we have Jesus in us.

Communion is sacred, therefore before or during mass we can go to confession to receive Jesus in the cleanest possible way. So as He gave himself up for our sins so must we receive Jesus with no or as little sin possible.

I believe that communion saves lives. I personally know that receiving Jesus everyday for 3 months and a half made me feel well, and it is when I am not receiving Jesus that I don't feel well, even though I know he is close to us. Communion makes us one flesh, the closest we can be to our Almighty Lord.

Jesus, the Bread from Heaven

Jesus is purity. He never sinned since He is God. He is purity and love. He is the one that condemns us in the end. Jesus said He is the bread of life from heaven, therefore going to Mass and receiving Jesus is of utmost importance. Even the Devil tried tempting Jesus in the desert to turn rocks into bread, He was hungry, but He resisted.

Jesus as a man did everything right. He did not sin. He obeyed His Father, Our Father in heaven and did everything as He wished. He resisted temptation to show us his example to overcome what is evil. He is the true manna or bread from heaven during the Eucharist (communion) and He gives himself completely body and blood for our salvation. He is our divine gift and even when He resurrected He gave us the divine gift of the Holy Spirit to spread the Great News and do not be afraid, God overcomes everything. Faith in Him alone we must have, He is our refuge and our strength.

Mother Mary - first Disciple of our Lord

Mother Mary is a perfect mother. All mother's should turn to her when they are having difficulty with their family or children. She is patient and kind and knows what it is to be a mother, knows what it is to suffer and pain. She witnessed her son die at the hands of men but knew with great faith the glory it would bring and the wonderousness of God that nothing is impossible with him. God is wonderful and he loves us to death that He sent his only Son to come down and save us and show us the way.

Mother Mary is a model disciple since she obeyed God's word and said yes to be Jesus' mother. Anything God asks of us we must do with great love. Being a disciple of Jesus and God is not only following in his footsteps but imitating his great love and be replicas of that love and doing what he says, the commandments too, and loving one another. Faith and action and footsteps. That is why Mother Mary was chosen to be the Queen of the World, her love for God surpassed all others in saying yes to God's plan to save the world and no other woman ever can compare to her virtue and purity. She is God's Mother and our Mother.

Great woman to lean on. Sometimes our own mother doesn't understand us, they have their problems and stresses in this life, kids encourage your mother's to turn to Mother Mary. She takes all our problems and encourages us and she makes our weight lighter like her Son. She handles our problems with care and makes everything OK in its due time. Many times she has been there for me in many times in my life. I am a witness of her great love for us. I used to watch Rosa de la Guadeloupe a wonderful Spanish program for teenagers and their daily problems, Mother Mary is always there for help. Teenage years are life's difficult moments and turning to Mother Mary she makes everything OK. She is there to protect, to guide, to love and show us God's great love for us Jesus, son of God, Redeemer of the world.

Jesus - The Resurrection

I was very fortunate to go to Jerusalem in 2015. The pictures I took most mysteriously disappeared but one was saved on my trip back from Jerusalem to Toronto. I saw the face of Jesus outside my window on the plane. He wants us to believe without seeing and so I ask the Lord how lucky I am to have seen his face and I hope to share that face that I saw up in the sky 30000 ft in the air, of my Savior and Lord Jesus. The resurrected Jesus that loves us so much that came back to tell us, that paid the ultimate price for our sins and saved us from eternal damnation. Thank you Jesus.

The resurrection is our assurance that there is more to this life. Whatever we do will be weighed in the end and will be decided by God. Whether we will rise to leave with Jesus or be burned in hell. God can do anything. He can resurrect the dead, no one else can do that. He is the living God, the God of life and light and His Word keeps on living in great faith. Believing in Him and believing in the one who sent Him and believing in the promise of life. Jesus is the Way, the Truth, and the Light. Personally I remember when Jack Layton passed and they were singing Rise Up and I really felt he would Rise Up. It was a touching ceremony, all of Canada felt his death and I hope we will all Rise Up one day with the Lord in great faith.

The resurrection of our Lord tells us we will see our loved ones again. It's a promise to rejoice and be happy that our Lord can do anything and through him anything is possible. He can do anything. Our deepest fears he consoles, our deepest pains he lifts up, our deepest despair he resurrects, nothing he can't do we have to just believe as he said.

Serving Our Lord, He came to serve

John 13 12-18 Jesus came to be an example. He did not come to be served but to serve, to teach us the way of the Lord. Even Peter was shocked when Jesus wanted to wash his feet but Jesus corrected him in telling him there is great joy in serving the Lord, Just joy in helping one another.

Jesus calls us to a Holy life. A Holy life he stated we must love one another to the point we'd die for one another, that is the truest divine love, since he came down for that. He describes us what Holy feels and looks like. It describes that love is serving and helping and Jesus died for everyone so we must love one another the same way.

Jesus wants us to be good Samaritans of love. In the parable he used the example of a man in need and asked which person was kindest to him. We should have good Samaritan cards with points redeemable at the end of our life with all the great deeds we have done for one another with the prize being heaven.

Jesus said to be first we have to be last. Jesus came to put straight all our misconceptions of love. He came to show us the true way to the Lord. It will not be easy but he is there with us and He has gone through it always accompanying us along the way along with the saints and angels. Our idea of love was first come first serve while Jesus said the opposite. See how much we needed Jesus, to show us the way, thank you Jesus!

Jesus the Way, the Truth and the Light

Jesus taught us the way to God's heavenly kingdom in his actions and words. He taught us how to love one another the way the Lord wants. He taught us the actions we must take to follow Jesus and be his faithful disciples.

Jesus is the Truth. There are many religions and many have touched truths. Buddhism teaches not to be attached to material things because they are a source of suffering and we can not serve 2 masters, money or God, because we will hate one and love the other. Hinduism teaches about sin when we do not live a good life we are punished but Jesus forgives us for our sins. Islam teaches peace and Jesus is our truest peace and teaches how to truly love. Judaism is still waiting for their Messiah while Christians are waiting for Jesus to come back. Jesus is the son of our Lord and he came down to save us from sins and our sinful lives and to teach us to love. Other religions have Christian qualities of sharing and caring but the truth is always Jesus. He came to be born in this world to tell us the truth of the other world, heaven.

Jesus is Light. Everything he proclaims gives sight to those that are blind, and understanding to those that don't. He is the light in the dark that keeps us hoping and seeing clearly. Jesus also makes our troubles light in that He loves us and tells us to come to Him for rest. All that are burdened he is light and helps our load feel lighter. Since the moment he is born he was light. The Star of David, a night light, guided the wisemen to him and when he resurrected angels were there at the tomb to say that Jesus resurrected and is with us. From beginning to end He is light just like in the beginning God created Light, He is light.

Redemption

God's greatest love for us is that He forgives us. He offers us an opportunity to change our lives. This sacrament is usually called Reconciliation. We receive it before communion as a symbol that to receive God entirely we must be completely clean from sins. Jesus gave the power to the Apostles to forgive sins as He does so that we can receive Jesus completely sinfree.

Reconciliation is also Jesus' great gift to us. Because we have sinned we have strayed away from God and Jesus came down to show us the path back to God. To repent from our sins and follow the Lord because the kingdom of God is near as John the Baptist proclaimed and making the path straight for our Lord to travel since Jesus is God.

Better to repeat now then after because we pass on according to our sins, we will be condemned. If we have sinned little or none we go to heaven. If we have sinned medium we go to purgatory where people can pray for us to go to heaven as St.Gertrude showed us in her prayer that saves 50000 souls when said. If we have sinned a lot we go to hell in
the fire that never ceases.

There are 7 capital sins: envy, lust, pride, greed, gluttony, sloth and anger.

And there are 10 commandments given to Moses for us to follow:
1-Thy shall believe in One God
2- Keep the Sunday holy.
3- Do not use God's name in vain.
4- Respect and honour your father and mother.
5- Do not lie.
6- Do not steal.
7- Do not kill.
8- Do not commit adultery.
9- Do not cover thy neighbors things.
10- Do not bare false witness.

When we are forgiven in confession we are clean, white, blank slate, radiating with God's grace. We are lost sheep returning home to the Lord. Reconciliation brings us closer to God, Jesus is our eternal Reconcilator.

Jesus, The Way of the Cross

For a time I used to do the way of the cross at St.Joseph's Oratory. Sometimes I'd practice doing it in the place of others, as a wife, as a mother, as a child, and imagine the weight on the shoulders that each bares and that we all have our crosses and are meant to help one another and carry ours. I always pictured doing a way of the cross with the love of my life, Eric.

Jesus takes all our worries, all our sorrows and carries them with him. He took all our sins and saved us. How joyous is our Lord that He saved us and we must only follow him. His footsteps are light because he already bared all the weight we just have to forget ourselves and follow him! How great is He who comes in the name of the Lord.

Let's try a practice of the 14 stations as children of the world today.

Station 1: Jesus is condemned.
Children bare your cross if you are rejected for your faith.

Station 2: Jesus picks up his cross.
Children bare the injuries and hardship of following Jesus.

Station 3: Jesus falls.
If you fall, God and his angels picks us up, try to pick up those that have fallen.

Station 4: Jesus and Mother Mary.
Mother Mary was Jesus' strength, make her yours too to continue.

Station 5: Simon.
Help one another with your crosses, if someone is stumbling hold them steady.

Station 6: Veronica
Cherish our Lord, his face and what he faced gives us strength and keeps us moving forward.

Station 7: Jesus falls a second time.
Saints and angels will keep you going if you fall again, Jesus holds us in his hands.

Station 8: Jesus and the people.
Let's get the whole world to follow Jesus.

Station 9: Jesus falls the last time.
He is our strength, behold the miracle after the third fall, if we must die for our faith, as martyrs in the past did, pray that in our darkest hour Jesus is there for us always. Let's lift Jesus up.

Station 10: Unrobes.
We may be humiliated for our faith, follow him.

Station 11: Nailed to the Cross.
We may endure pain for our faith, follow him.

Station 12: Jesus on the cross.
We may die for our faith, follow him.

Station 13: Jesus in Mary's arms.
Mother Mary holds us and carries us to the Lord we are precious, her son paid the price for us.

Station 14: Jesus in the tomb.
Behold the greatest mystery of the world revealed in 3 days. In the end of time we will resurrect thanks to God. Nothing is impossible to God!

Rosary

St.Dominic was the first saint that created the rosary as a form of prayer and dedication to Mother Mary. St. Pope John Paul 2 added the necessity of praying the rosary everyday and even added the Luminous Mysteries on Thursdays to add extra devotion to Mother Mary of God.

The Rosary starts with the Apostle's Creed, then an Our Father, then 3 Hail Marys and a Glory Be. Then depending on the day there are 5 mysteries to meditate upon. Monday and Saturdays are the Joyous mysteries: The Annunciation, the Visitation, the Nativity, the Presentation and Finding Jesus in the Temple.

Tuesdays and Fridays are the Sorrowful mysteries: the Garden of Gethsemane, Jesus is beaten, Jesus is struck with a rod and humiliated, Jesus falls and Jesus dies.

On Wednesdays and Sundays are the Glorious mysteries: the Resurrection, the Ascension, the gift of the Holy Spirit, the Assumption and Mary is made Queen of Heaven and Earth and lastly the Luminous mysteries on Thursdays: the Baptism of Jesus, the miracle of Cana, the Mount of the Beatitudes, the Transfiguration and the Eucharist. Depending on the day, an Our Father is said, then the Mystery, followed by 10 Hail Marys and a Glory Be and an Oh my Jesus forgive us our sins, save us from the fire of hell especially those most need of your mercy. An intention of prayer can be said after the mystery.

It is recommended to recite the rosary one time a day in our Christian lives to pray for others and our own intentions. It takes about 15 minutes to recite. Many can start a prayer group and recite together one time a week to practice and socialize and gather strength and support together.

One of my first and foremost memories of my grandma, my mom's mom, is her rosary in her hand praying. My other grandma prays a lot too but the other image marked me. She used to go to bed after everyone else praying the rosary in her hand. I knew from young that praying has lots of positive power in it. I recite the rosary twice a day but some saints like Padre Pio who performed miraculous things recited the rosary 30 times a day. Prayer is powerful.

The Bible

The Bible is God's spoken word to us through the Holy Spirit through individuals that have grasped that message throughout history. In the Old Testament, it talks of creation, these truths were revealed through the Holy Spirit to certain individuals. The prophets in the Old Testament usually warned the people to change their ways. Prophets also spoke of Jesus the Messiah. Jesus completes the Bible, since He was the awaited king, Son of God, that died for us.

The New Testament speaks of Jesus' miracles of healings and preaching. He made everything new. His existence changed the world and He has existed since the beginning of time like His Father, God. And will return at the end of time on Judgement Day as revealed in the Revelations by one of His own apostle's John.

Every word in the New and Old Testament is sacred since they are considered words of the spoken by God to individuals to reveal truths through the Holy Spirit. The Bible is about God and his Holy messages about the past, present and future.

Jesus is in all of us, we must be like kids

There is an image of our Lord in all of us and we must always remember that God came to teach us love and bring us closer to Him. His love is eternal, His love is unconditional, His love is everlasting and endures forever.

Jesus wants us to be like children. When we are children we are innocent and in bliss, we love God earnestly and lovingly like we should. We don't question we just want to play and enjoy all day and have fun, innocent fun. As we get older things change, we are adults, we question things more, we have responsibilities, we forget to have fun. We must have great faith.

Jesus said we must welcome little children as though they were Him because He is pure and innocent and also God's son. Children are beautiful and that's God's gift to us His own child. So small, so beautiful wit the biggest mission in the world that he completed with great faith. We as adults must not forget we were children too and keep in touch with our child side to be closer to God who calls us all back to Him.

As Christians we are salt and light Jesus said. Salt adds flavor and light is put on a shelf for all the world to see and Jesus enlightened our hearts, our minds and our lives through His ways and enriches our lives with flavor and preserves it from going bad but keeps us good for longer. Jesus is the Light of the World.

What did Jesus dying on the cross mean?

Jesus dying on the cross is about saving the world. He redeemed us through His Words, His Action and His Faith.

His words are everlasting words, they come straight from heaven. Every word as Peter said were words of Eternal Life. Now that we don't see Jesus anymore, we have faith that He will return and hold onto His promise and His words. We must remember to keep His word alive in our everyday and t reflect and make us follow His example and footsteps.

His action taught us love. The embodiment of love is Jesus. He gave us His body to eat, His blood to drink and promised that's all we need for Eternal Life. His body still heals us even after death and resurrection. His action taught us love, he preached the Good News, he healed as many people and keeps healing people, he taught in the synagogues for everyone, he expelled demons and taught us how to love one another in everything he did. His Way is the Truth, the Way and the Light.

Through his example we are saved. He is and was God on Earth and came to show us the way to our Heavenly Father, to always have faith in Him because seeing Him is seeing the Father. Be not afraid, His famous words that resonate on fear of death, there is resurrection. We have to live by His example always and follow His footsteps to meet Him again in faith.

St. Joseph, Protector of the Church and Mother Mary, Mother of the Church

In Canada, St. Joseph is considered Protector of the Church since He fathered Jesus on Earth and led Him from a child to older to follow in the ways of the Lord. Even the Son of God needed a Father to lead the way and Christ born as an infant like each one of us, children of God, in a way showed us that the church will guide our children to God. Priests that consecrate their lives to God are considered Fathers. They themselves, in the Catholic faith, can not marry or have children but we are considered their children since they shepherd us to God and protect us.

Mother Mary is considered too for protecting the church. Mothers and Fathers are naturally very protective of their children and they desire the best of them to put everything in the hands of God and they are in good hands. We, on the other hand, put the church in the hands of Mother Mary and St. Joseph so that we know in divine hands we can not lose sight of God and to keep our faith strong. We acknowledge our weaknesses to find out what God asks of us through sin so then if we pray with great faith our mistakes can be forgiven ad lifted and our faith guided by someone stronger who can do more.

Mother Mary gave birth to our Lord, that saved us and in essence gave birth to the church since we adore and follow Him. She guides our ways to him, she consoles us in our moments of despair since she had great faith in Jesus and God's plan for humanity. Through her and her intercession many are saved and brought closer to God. She gathers her children as our Mother. Jesus said when he was at the cross that Mary is our Mother. She reconciled the world through Jesus and even as we await Jesus' return yet he is always wit us, she was taken to heaven by Jesus and made Queen of Heaven and Earth, so her intercession is in the greatest faith. With God there is no fear, only joy even with our deepest sorrows that she had suffered we rejoice in the resurrection, we just need to have faith.

Her image and model is impeccable, woman of highest ranks, majesty and she is love. She protects us and guides the church through its evolving times to stay faithful and virtuous and always forgiving and asking for forgiveness. She is our Heavenly Mother and loves us so much and our Lord's dearest Mother.

7 Heavenly virtues

They are the opposite of the capital sins. The 7 Heavenly virtues are kindness, humility, patience, diligence, temperance, charity and chastity.

Kindness is showing that you care for others, think of others, are considerate of others feelings. Kindness to yourself is loving yourself and making sure that you eat right and exercise and keep yourself healthy.

Humility is not boosting that we are the best but keep it to ourselves. Humility is also not choosing the best place at a party or dinner but rather waiting to be shown one's seat. Jesus asks us to be humble and show humility that way we will be lifted up rather than the other way around.

Patience is taking your time with yourself and with others. Everything in its due time no need to rush. When we are patient we are calm and ready to give as much love as is needed to any situation.

Diligence is working hard. We need to keep busy doing good things for our Lord because we don't know the hour when we must go back to heaven.

Temperance teaches us moderation. All pleasures like food, drink, sex, travel, shopping must be in moderation or we risk dependencies on pleasures which can lead to sin. If we can control ourselves we win against sin.

Charity is a beautiful virtue, it's about sharing with others what we have. Nobody has everything, we are incomplete without God and one another. Charity can be giving our time, giving our efforts, giving our money, and giving our knowledge to others.

Chastity is remaining abstinent, without sexual relations, with others. When one waits till they are married to make love with their partner it is the most beautiful gift you can offer. Many try before and end up disappointed and with a broken-heart. The Virgin Mother Mary was chaste and you can pray to her to keep you chaste.

7 gifts of the Holy Spirit

The seven gifts of the Holy Spirit are wisdom, understanding, counsel, fortitude, knowledge, piety, and fear of the Lord. ...

I used to be a catechist and my only group of children that I taught were receiving their confirmation that year and received these gifts. I was happy to be a part of it.

Wisdom is the gift that King Solomon, from the Old Testament, prayed for and the Lord blessed him with great wisdom. Wisdom is above knowledge or having a lot of experience and making a better decision about something.

Understanding is the gift that the psychology departments use the most. They understand their patients and clients clearly and act accordingly. We also understand our friends and offer sound advice to them. When there are problems we need understanding to resolve it. Sometimes we need to view a problem from different perspectives to fully understand it.

Counsel is similar to understanding in that it is advice offered to any given situation. Good advice.

Fortitude is another word for courage. When the Apostles received the Holy Spirit from Jesus, courage was essential for them to preach to all nations as Jesus said. Courage gives one the bravery to do outstanding things, things that we'd otherwise be too afraid to do. He always told us Be not afraid and so we must not in preaching the Word of God and doing good.

Knowledge is knowing things and understanding them. It is an awareness of ourselves and others around us and gaining facts and information about them. When you know someone well, you may not love everything about them sometimes but you accept them and love them.

Piety is a quality of being religious. Nuns and monks have piety, they have chosen their vocation. You can devote your life to God without becoming a priest or nun too. Devotion to our Lord is showing piety.

Fear of the Lord is that we are always aware that God is God and He has the final say to our soul. He has the power and we are here to praise Him and love Him and fear Him.

Sins

The 7 capital sins are envy, pride, wrath, sloth, gluttony, lust and greed.

Sins are bad and they keep us away from God. Luckily God forgives our sins through the sacrament of reconciliation or penance. Thanks to the priests we are reconciled to God and we are like blank slates afterwards since he forgives our sins for us.

Envy is the sin of wanting what others have whether material things or people. Sometimes we may be envious of a family and wish to have what they have. Or sometimes our friend or neighbor may have a toy or a dress or a shirt we like as well but can't afford it. The opposite of envy is kindness and sharing with others.

Pride is when we think we are better than others and are arrogant towards others. Lucifer was the most beautiful angel of God but he didn't want to serve God anymore he wanted to be better than God, his sin was pride. We are born equal and though we have different gifts we must be humble about them and show humility. That is the opposite of pride.

Wrath is when we get angry and have no control over what we say and do. We must always remain in control because what we say can hurt others physically, verbally, emotionally, etc. The opposite of wrath is patience.

Sloth is when we feel lazy to do anything. Like the animal the sloth takes its time and is sluggish all day. God wants us to keep busy doing good things for others and for ourselves. We shouldn't be sleeping all day, or watching tv, we should be diligent and that's the opposite of sloth.

Gluttony is wanting too much sex, drink, food and pleasure in this life. We become dependent on these things to be happy but God wants us love things in moderation and not to become addicted to pleasures. The opposite of gluttony is temperance.

Lust is uncontrollable sexual desire. Like gluttony we must remain in control of our desires. All pleasure can lead to dependency and sin. We must be stronger than the addiction. The best way to control lust is to be chaste which is the opposite.

Greed is a terrible sin like the others. Like the Grinch wanted all the toys for him and stole them all in the Christmas special. There are people in this life that never have enough money, shoes, clothes. If we'd just share and give to charity everyone would have enough.

7 sacraments

The 7 sacraments are baptism, communion, confirmation, reconciliation, marriage, Holy orders and anointing of the sick.

Baptism is when we become children of God. Many are baptized when they are babies but others new to the faith get baptized when they are older. We inherit Godparents when we get baptized. The priest pours water on our heads and says it in the name of the Father, Son and Holy Spirit just like John the Baptist did and then we are baptized.

Communion is usually given at the young age of 7-8 years old but it can be given at any age as long as you received the sacrament of baptism. It is then that we are able to receive Jesus in the Holy Eucharist. He is the Bread of Life and He feeds us with His Body during Holy Communion.

Confirmation is usually given at age 10- 11 years old but it can be given at any age as long as you received the sacraments of baptism and first communion. Confirmation is when we receive the Holy Spirit and it's 7 gifts. If we are a boy we chose another Godfather and if we are a girl we chose a Godmother. It commemorates Pentecost when Jesus gave his apostles the Holy Spirit to preach God's Good News. Usually the Bishop gives us the Holy Spirit.

Reconciliation is when we return back to God also known as Penance. It is then that we profess our sins to a priest and he intersects with God's forgiveness. He tells us how many our fathers and hail Marys for our penance for our sins. We are then clean slates.

Marriage is when two people want to unite their lives forever and promise to do so in front of God. If the marriage doesn't work out it can be annulled but usually it's till death do us the part.

Holy Orders is when one has a calling to becoming a nun, monk, or priesthood. God has called them not to marry but to give their life to serving others and him.

Anointing of the sick is our last sacrament. It is usually given when one is about to die. The priest gives a final blessing to the person that prepares them to leave this world and enter God's kingdom.

Saint and Prophets

In the Old Testament we don't hear too much about saints, but prophets. Prophets are Holy people chosen by God to announce God's message to the people. Many are in the Old Testament Bible. Examples are Hosea, Ezekiel, Elijah, Moses, Noah, Amos, Jeremiah, Isaiah, Haberkkuk, Zephariah, Jonah, Zechariah and many more. Each had a personal message from God to give to his people to change their way or destruction will come, and luckily many of the times destruction was avoided. Except for Noah's case, the whole world was destroyed and made new through him and his family and the animals in the 40 days flood.

In only New Testament prophet we know of is John the Baptist. He was predicted in Isaiah to be preparing the way for the Savior, our Messiah, Jesus Christ. It was his cousin the Great Savior. When Jesus was baptized by him heaven opened up to reveal God's voice that he was pleased with His son and was very pleased with him. John the Baptist had many followers and disciples and they all followed Jesus after His baptism to do as Jesus wants and asked of them.

Saints on the other hand are followers of Christ that have made their lives holy for God. To make one's life holy one can pray a lot, can fast a lot, the body is your temple of holiness. Once the body is holy it can do a lot of miracles and heartfelt good, like heal the sick, take out demons, and preaching and teaching about God's kingdom. Anybody can become a saint while prophets were chosen by God. To be a saint requires that after you die, 2 miracles have to be attributed by your intervention. First you are blessed, then you are venerated and then you are canonized and become a saint. This may take years. Body parts of a saint are usually kept in churches or cathedrals and they are called relics.

Jesus our Savior and the Trinity

God the Father is the Creator of the world but even when He existed His son Jesus existed and even when both existed, existed the Holy Spirit. The Holy Spirit was our gift from Jesus after He died and resurrected and Jesus is our gift from God on Christmas that saved us from sin and redeemed us both to God from our Original sin. Together all 3 make One Trinity, God is but 1 in 3 parts and this profound mystery is still pondered today as are many of God's mysteries.

The Holy Spirit existed even before because it was the Holy Spirit that impregnated the Virgin Mother Mary with Jesus. John the Baptist, Jesus' cousin, also claimed that Jesus would baptize with the Holy Spirit.

In the Transfiguration, Luke 9:28-37, the voice of the Lord resonates through the clouds that Jesus is God's son and He wants us to listen to Him.

Jesus gives us His gifts in John 20:19-30. The Holy Spirit is often compared to a gentle white dove and tongues of flames because we are suddenly filled with zest and love for the Lord. We want to risk our lives proclaiming his message in various languages and we are filled with faith. The Holy Spirit can do anything and Jesus gave all that as a gift. Jesus went through locked doors to give us the gift and to help others have faith and proclaim God's great message of hope for all and to open the doors of faith in our hearts and minds.

During confirmation we all receive the Holy Spirit. Each gift enhances our knowing and understanding of our Lord. Essentially, He is always so close to us and wants us to be the same with the right understanding of who He really is. God loves us to death and proved it with Jesus and wants us to love one another deeply and honestly like the Holy Spirit so that our hearts, minds and souls will belong to God.

MIX
Papier aus verantwortungsvollen Quellen
Paper from responsible sources
FSC® C105338

Printed by Books on Demand GmbH, Norderstedt / Germany